Microsoft® Word®
Mail Merge
The Step-By-Step Guide

C.J. Benton

ISBN-10: 1539916081
ISBN-13: 978-1539916086

Other Books Available By This Author:

Table of Contents

CHAPTER 1
How To Use This Book

This book can be used as a tutorial or quick reference guide and is intended for users who are just getting started with the Mail Merge functionality in Microsoft® Word®.

While this book is intended for beginners, it does assume you already know how to create, open, and save a Microsoft® Word® document, and have a general familiarity with the Word® toolbar.

All of the examples in this book use **Microsoft® Word® 2013**, however, most of the functionality can be applied with Microsoft® Word® version 2007 or later.

Please always **back-up your work** and **save often**. A good best practice when attempting any new functionality is to **create a copy of the original Word document** and implement your changes on the copied document. Should anything go wrong, you then have the original file to fall back on. Please see the diagram below.

Diagram 1:

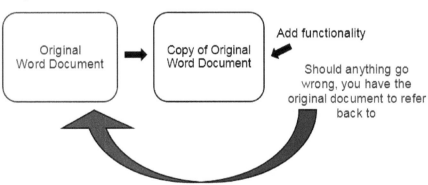

This book is structured into 3 parts. Part one focuses on the Mail Merge fundamentals, how to *setup a Data Source file*, *creating a letter*, and *viewing the merged letters before printing*. This section also includes an example on how to create mailing labels.

Part 2 reviews how to utilize data contained in Excel® to create a Mail Merge document using a billing invoice example with currency and percent values.

Lastly, part 3 discusses how to generate Outlook® email messages using Mail Merge and incorporating fields contained in the Outlook® Contacts feature.

The table below is a summary of the functionality and features detailed in each section:

PART 1 – MAIL MERGE BASICS	
Chapters 3 - 4	1. Form letters 2. Mailing labels
PART 2 –MAIL MERGE WITH MS EXCEL	
Chapter 5	3. Creating invoices & incorporating Dynamic Data Exchange (DDE)
PART 3 – MAIL MERGE WITH OUTLOOK®	
Chapter 6	4. Email messages with a Data Source file 5. Email messages with Outlook® Contacts fields

CHAPTER 2
Mail Merge Process Overview

What is Mail Merge?

Mail Merge is a feature within Microsoft® Word® that allows you to create mass communications in which specific sections can be tailored to individuals or groups. Examples include:

- Letters *(i.e. to customers or employees)*
- Advertisements, Promotional, or Marketing Materials
- Invoices
- Emails *(i.e. to customers or employees)*
- Mailing Labels

One of the main benefits of Mail Merge is you're able to take advantage of existing lists of customer or employee data, and can customize the communication medium without having to manually change each correspondence. The Mail Merge feature saves time and reduces the chance of errors occurring when someone must physically type or modify each message.

Since Mail Merge is part of the Microsoft® Office® product suite, it interfaces with other Microsoft® Office® products such as:

- Microsoft® Access®
- Microsoft® Excel®
- Microsoft® Outlook®

This association provides the ability to maintain customer or employee data separately and adapt each communication with minimal effort.

What are the main parts of Mail Merge?
All Mail Merge communication consists of three parts:

1. **Data Source:** The Data Source contains the individual information to customize the communication. Items such as customer or employee data.

2. **Document Type:** The Document Type contains *both* the fields that are to be merged *(individualized information)* as well as the text that does not change. Document Types include *Documents (i.e. letters, invoices, recipes etc.)*, *Emails*, *Mailing Labels*, or *Envelopes*.

3. **Merged Document**: The Merged Document is the *output of merge*. For example, the personalized finished Letter, Label, or Email tailored for each recipient.

Conceptual diagram of the Mail Merge process:

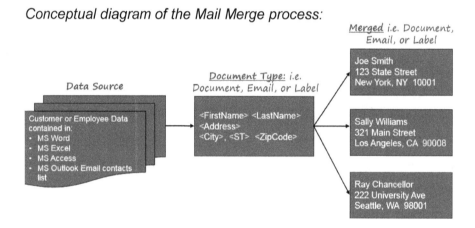

CHAPTER 3

Form Letters

For our first example using the Mail Merge feature we'll create a form letter to communicate an upcoming employee event.

The following will guide you through the basic Mail Merge functionality, including how to *setup a Data Source file, creating the letter*, and *viewing the merged letters before printing*.

CREATING THE DATA SOURCE FILE

STEP-BY-STEP EXAMPLE:

1. Open Microsoft® Word® and create a new blank Word® document **(CTRL + N)**

2. From the Ribbon select **INSERT : TABLE** 7 columns and 4 rows

3. Create a new folder in Windows® Explorer® called: **C:\MailMergeTraining**
   a. Open **Windows Explorer**
   b. Select the drive **C:**
   c. Click **'New Folder'**

4. Name the newly created folder: **MailMergeTraining**

5. Save and name the Word® file **(CTRL + S)** name it **MailMergeDataSource.docx** in the newly created folder

6. Enter the following headings in the first row of the table:
    - FirstName *(make sure no space between First & Name)*
    - LastName *(make sure no space between Last & Name)*
    - Address
    - City
    - ST
    - ZipCode *(make sure no space between Zip & Code)*
    - DOB *(Date Of Birth)*

FirstName	LastName	Address	City	ST	ZipCode	DOB

Add the source data:

FirstName	LastName	Address	City	ST	ZipCode	DOB
Joe	Smith	123 State Street	New York	NY	10001	05/01/1975
Sally	Williams	321 Main Street	Los Angeles	CA	90008	11/18/1985
Ray	Chancellor	222 University Ave	Seattle	WA	98001	02/25/1969

7. Enter the following under **FirstName**:
    - Joe
    - Sally
    - Ray

8. Enter the following under **LastName**:
    - Smith
    - Williams
    - Chancellor

9. Enter the following under **Address**:
    - 123 State Street
    - 321 Main Street
    - 222 University Ave

10. Enter the following under **City**:
    - New York
    - Los Angeles
    - Seattle

11. Enter the following under **ST**:
    - NY
    - CA
    - WA

12. Enter the following under **ZipCode**:
- 10001
- 90008
- 98001

13. Enter the following under **DOB**:
- 05/01/1975
- 11/18/1985
- 02/25/1969

14. Save **(CTRL + S)** and **Close** the file

CREATING THE LETTER DOCUMENT

1. Create a new blank Word® document **(CTRL + N)**

2. Type the following text information:

> 19 September 2016
>
> Dear :
>
> Open Enrollment begins **01 October 2016** through **31 October 2016**. To change your elections, logon via the company benefits website and enter the following information:
> ```
>         First Name:
>          Last Name:
>            Address:
>                DOB:
> ```
>
> Thank you,
> HR Department

3. Save the form letter to: **C:\MailMergeTraining**

4. Name the letter: **'FormLetter'**

5. From the Ribbon select **MAILINGS : Start Mail Merge : Step-by-Step Mail Merge Wizard...**

The following wizard should now appear on your screen

6. Under **'Select document type'** verify the **'Letters'** radio button is selected and click **'Next: Starting document'**

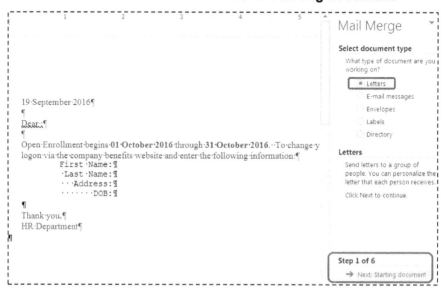

7. Click 'Next: Select recipients'

8. Under 'Use an existing list', click the 'Browse...' option

9. When prompted, open the **C:\MailMergeTraining** folder

10. Select the file: **'MailMergeDataSource.docx'**

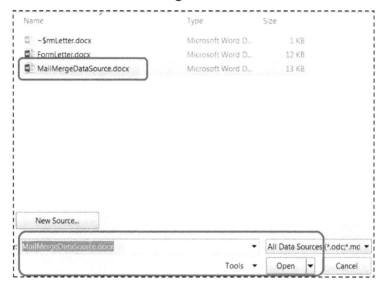

11. Click the **'Open'** button

The following prompt will appear:

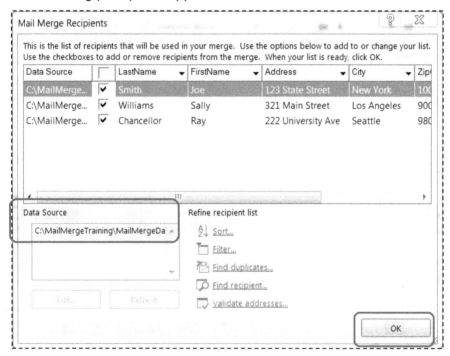

12. Click the **'OK'** button

13. Place your cursor in from front of the word **'Dear'**

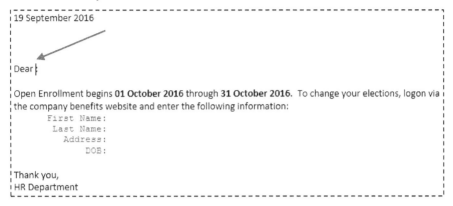

14. From the **'MAILINGS'** tab select the **'Insert Merge Field'** drop-down box

15. Select **'FirstName'** (*should be inserted after the word 'Dear'*)

16. After **'FirstName'** press your **'Spacebar'** on your keyboard

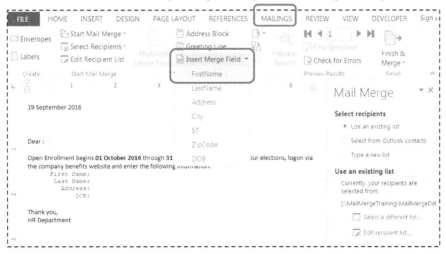

17. From the **'Insert Merge Field'** drop-down box Select
    'LastName' *(should be inserted after FirstName and space)*

18. Place your cursor after the words `First Name:`

19. Add a space *(press the spacebar on your keyboard)*

20. From the **'Insert Merge Field'** drop-down box select
    'FirstName'

21. Repeats steps 17 - 19 for fields:

    - `Last Name: «LastName»`
    - `Address: «Address»`
    - `DOB: «DOB»`

The **'FormLetter'** document should look similar to the following:

19 September 2016

Dear «FirstName» «LastName»:

Open Enrollment begins **01 October 2016** through **31 October 2016**. To change your elections, logon via the company benefits website and enter the following information:
```
    First Name: «FirstName»
     Last Name: «LastName»
       Address: «Address»
           DOB: «DOB»
```
Thank you,
HR Department

22. Save the file **(CTRL + S)**

THE SQL PROMPT *(opening a document containing merged fields)*

After saving and closing a document that contains merged fields, and then re-opening that file, you're *linking* to a data source, Microsoft® refers to this as "database." As such, when opening a document that contains merged fields you'll receive the following prompt, simply **click 'Yes'**, to proceed with opening the document.

MERGING THE DOCUMENT

1. With the **'FormLetter'** document open, select the **'MAILINGS'** tab

2. Select the **'Finish & Merge'** drop-down box and then **'Edit Individual Documents…'**

The following prompt should appear:

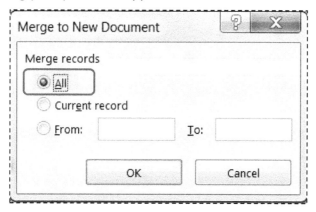

3. If not already selected, select the '**<u>A</u>ll**' radio button

4. Click the '**OK**' button

A new Word document should now be created, note the personalized information:

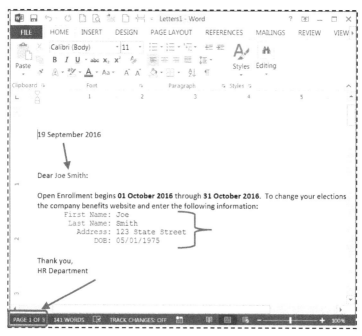

Review the **'Letters1'** merged document, if the results are as you expected them to be, you may *rename and save* the file or *print out* each letter for distribution.

HELPFUL TIPS

To easily see your document's merged fields, click the button **'Highlight Merge Fields'**. This will highlight each merged field.

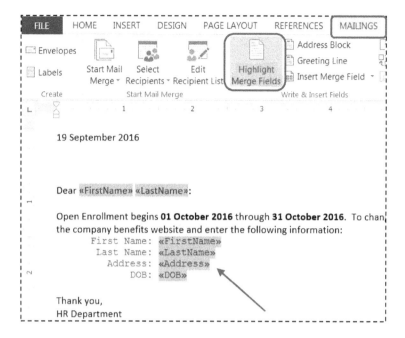

Before generating the merged document, you may preview the merged records, by clicking the button **'Preview Results'**. This is especially useful if you're incorporating many merge fields or generating a large number of merged records.

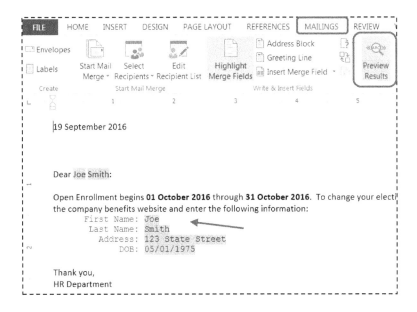

19 September 2016

Dear Joe Smith:

Open Enrollment begins **01 October 2016** through **31 October 2016**. To change your electi
the company benefits website and enter the following information:

```
First Name: Joe
 Last Name: Smith
   Address: 123 State Street
       DOB: 05/01/1975
```

Thank you,
HR Department

CHAPTER 4

Mailing Labels

In this chapter we learn how to create mailing labels. To save time we'll use the existing Data Source file created in <u>Chapter 3</u>.

You may complete this exercise even if you don't have labels for printing.

STEP-BY-STEP EXAMPLE:

CREATING THE LABEL DOCUMENT

1. Open Microsoft® Word® and create a new blank Word® document **(CTRL + N)**

2. From the Ribbon select **MAILINGS : Start Mail Merge : Step-by-Step Mail Merge <u>W</u>izard…**

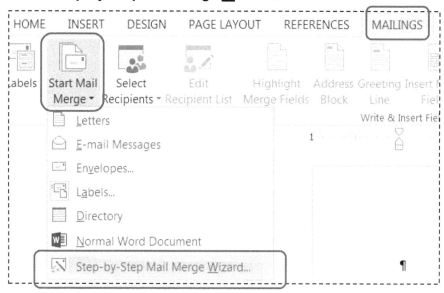

The following wizard should now appear on your screen

3. Under **'Select document type'**, choose the **'Labels'** radio button

4. Click **'Next: Starting document'**

5. Under **'Change document layout'** select **'Label options…'**

6. Choose the appropriate label option for your country and product number. *You may complete this exercise even if you don't have labels for printing.*

7. Click the **'OK'** button

8. Click **'Next: Select recipients'**

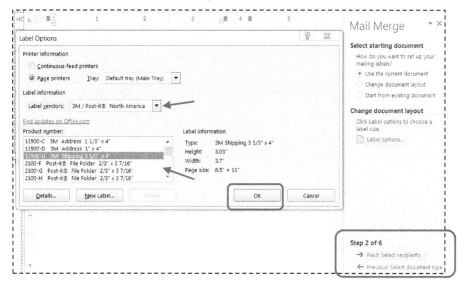

9. Under **'Use an existing list',** click the **'Browse...'** option

10. When prompted, open the **C:\MailMergeTraining** folder

11. Select the file: **'MailMergeDataSource.docx'**

12. Click the **'Open'** button

The following prompt will appear:

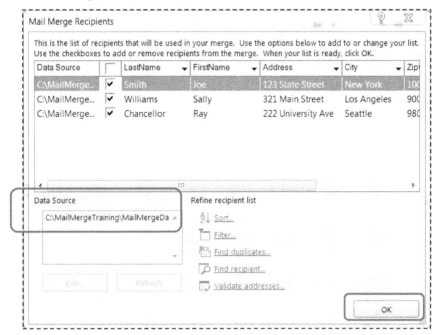

13. Click the **'OK'** button

You should now see a result *similar* to the following:

14. To assist with readability, from the Ribbon select **TABLE TOOLS : DESIGN**

15. Using the **'Borders'** drop-down box select **'View Gridlines'**

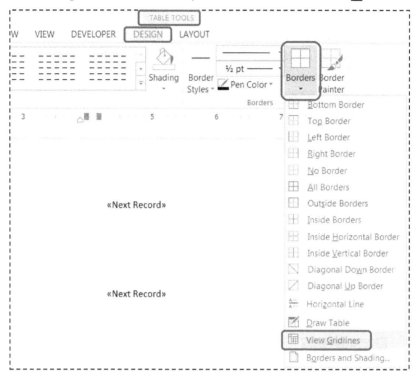

16. Place your cursor in the first label box.

17. From the **'MAILINGS'** tab select the **'Insert Merge Field'** drop-down box, select **'FirstName'**

18. After **'FirstName'** press your **'Spacebar'** on your keyboard

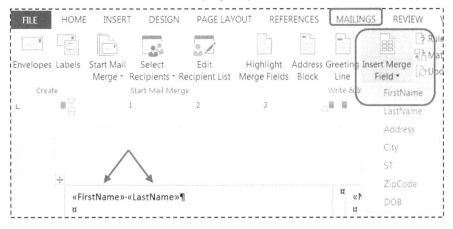

19. From the **'Insert Merge Field'** drop-down box select **'LastName'** *(should be inserted after FirstName and space)*

20. On a new line, under «FirstName» «LastName» select the **'Insert Merge Field'** drop-down box and **'Address'**

21. On a new line, under «Address» select the **'Insert Merge Field'** drop-down box and **'City'**

22. After **'City'** insert a comma (,) and press your **'Spacebar'** on your keyboard

23. From the **'Insert Merge Field'** drop-down box select **'ST'** *(should be inserted after City, and space)*

24. After **'ST'** press your **'Spacebar'** on your keyboard twice

25. From the **'Insert Merge Field'** drop-down box select **'ZipCode'** *(should be inserted after ST and two spaces)*

26. Click 'Next: Arrange your labels'

27. Under 'Replicate labels' click the button 'Update all labels'

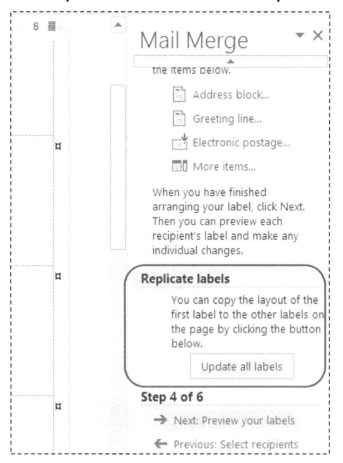

28. Save the labels to: **C:\MailMergeTraining**

29. Name the labels: **'Labels.docx'**

THE SQL PROMPT *(opening a document containing merged fields)*

After saving and closing a label document that contains merged fields, and then re-opening the label file, you're *linking* to a data source, Microsoft® refers to this as "database." As such, when opening a label file that contains merged fields you'll receive the following prompt, simply **click 'Yes'**, to proceed with opening the labels.

MERGING THE LABELS

1. With the **'Labels'** document open, select the **'MAILINGS'** tab

2. Select the **'Finish & Merge'** drop-down box and then **'Edit Individual Documents…'**

The following prompt should appear:

3. If not already selected, select the '**All**' radio button
4. Click the '**OK**' button

A new label document should now be created. Review the labels, if the results are as you expected them to be, you may *rename and save* the file or *print out* the labels for mailing.

CHAPTER 5

Invoice example using Microsoft® Excel® as the Data Source

Now let's build on the previous lessons learned in this book by creating a Data Source file in an application other than Microsoft® Word®. Often data such as customer, employee, or sales information is stored in databases like Microsoft® Access® or in spreadsheets.

In this chapter we'll create a Microsoft® Excel® spreadsheet Data Source file with sales data and use it to generate a Mail Merge invoice document.

To save time we'll re-use the records contained in the **'MailMergeDataSource.docx'** file.

> In order to complete this exercise, you will need
> **Microsoft® Excel®** installed on your computer.

DYNAMIC DATA EXCHANGE (DDE)

In this Mail Merge example we will be using **currency** and **percentage formats in Microsoft® Excel®**. In order for Microsoft® Word® to retain these formats we must use what Microsoft® calls **Dynamic Data Exchange (DDE)**, basically we're going to tell Word® the type of file formatting to apply based on the Data Source. If we DID NOT use DDE the following would result:

FORMAT	EXCEL®	WORD® *(without using DDE)*
Currency	$5.00	5
Percentage	10%	0.10000000000000001

1. From the **Microsoft® Word®** Ribbon select the **'FILE'** tab

2. Select **'Options'**

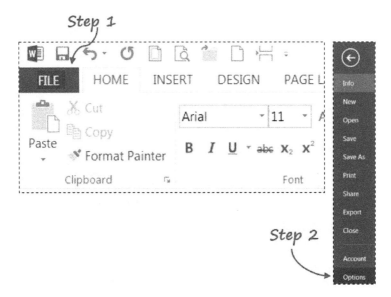

3. Select **'Advanced'** and scroll down to the section **'General'**

4. Click the box **'Confirm file format conversion on open'**

5. Click the **'OK'** button

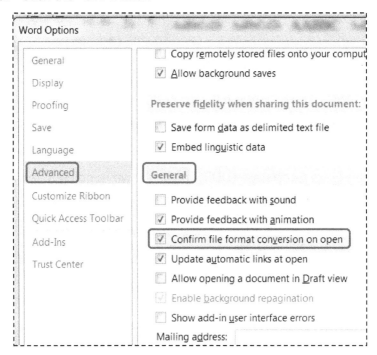

6. **You may need to reboot your computer after completing this step**

CREATING THE DATA SOURCE FILE

STEP-BY-STEP EXAMPLE:

1. Open **Microsoft® Excel®** and create a new blank Excel® spreadsheet **(CTRL + N)**

2. Open the **C:\MailMergeTraining** folder and select the file: **'MailMergeDataSource.docx'**

3. With the **Microsoft® Word®** file **'MailMergeDataSource.docx'** open press **(CTRL+A)** on your keyboard to *'Select All'* contents or:
   - From the Ribbon select the **'HOME'** tab
   - Click the **'Editing'** button
   - From drop-down box choose **'Select All'**

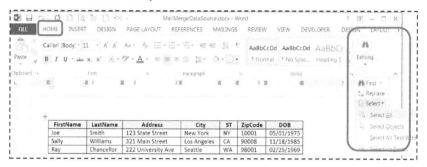

4. After selecting all, copy the contents, by pressing **(CTRL+C)** on your keyboard or:
   - From the Ribbon select the **'HOME'** tab
   - Click the **'Copy'** button

5. Return to the newly created blank **Excel®** spreadsheet and place your cursor in cell **'A1'** and press **(CTRL+V)** on your keyboard or:

    - From the Ribbon select the **'HOME'** tab
    - Click the **'Paste'** button

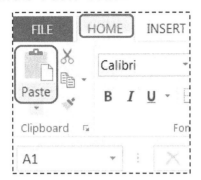

A spreadsheet similar to the following should now be displayed:

	A	B	C	D	E	F	G
1	FirstName	LastName	Address	City	ST	ZipCode	DOB
2	Joe	Smith	123 State Street	New York	NY	10001	5/1/1975
3	Sally	Williams	321 Main Street	Los Angeles	CA	90008	########
4	Ray	Chancellor	222 University Ave	Seattle	WA	98001	########

6. Save the spreadsheet to: **C:\MailMergeTraining**

7. Name the spreadsheet: **'MailMergeExcelDataSource.xlsx'**

8. You may adjust the spreadsheet *column width* and *row height* to improve readability

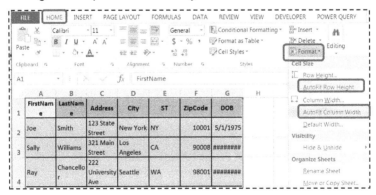

9. Place your cursor in cell '**H1**' and type '**Purchase**'

10. Place your cursor in cell '**I1**' and type '**Price**'

11. Place your cursor in cell '**J1**' and type '**Discount**'

12. Highlight cells '**J2:J4**' and format as a percent (%)

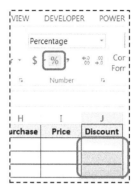

13. Enter the number 10 in cells '**J2:J4**'

14. Enter the following in cells:

   - '**H2**' type '**Apples**'
   - '**H3**' type '**Oranges**'
   - '**H4**' type '**Mangos**'

15. Enter the following in cells:

   - '**I2**' type '**5**'
   - '**I3**' type '**6**'
   - '**I4**' type '**7**'

16. Highlight cells '**I2:I4**' and format in your preferred currency, in this example I will use the **£ British Pound**

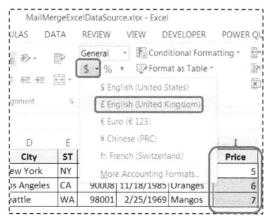

The spreadsheet should now appear *similar* to the following:

	A	B	C	D	E	F	G	H	I	J
1	FirstName	LastName	Address	City	ST	ZipCode	DOB	Purchase	Price	Discount
2	Joe	Smith	123 State Street	New York	NY	10001	5/1/1975	Apples	£ 5.00	10%
3	Sally	Williams	321 Main Street	Los Angeles	CA	90008	11/18/1985	Oranges	£ 6.00	10%
4	Ray	Chancellor	222 University Ave	Seattle	WA	98001	2/25/1969	Mangos	£ 7.00	10%

17. Save **(CTRL + S)** and **Close** the file

CREATING THE INVOICE DOCUMENT

1. Create a new blank Word® document **(CTRL + N)**

2. Type the following text information:

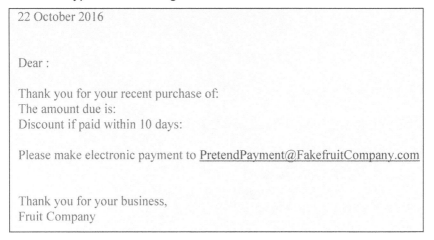

22 October 2016

Dear :

Thank you for your recent purchase of:
The amount due is:
Discount if paid within 10 days:

Please make electronic payment to PretendPayment@FakefruitCompany.com

Thank you for your business,
Fruit Company

3. Save the form letter to: **C:\MailMergeTraining**

4. Name the letter: **'FormInvoice.docx'**

5. From the Ribbon select **MAILINGS : Select Recipients : Use an Existing List...**

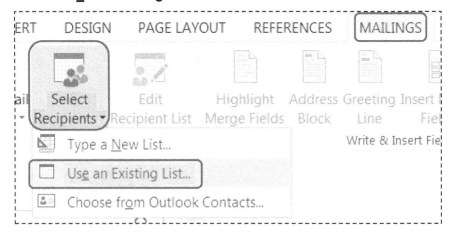

6. When prompted, open the **C:\MailMergeTraining** folder

7. Select the file: '**MailMergeExcelDataSource.xlsx**'

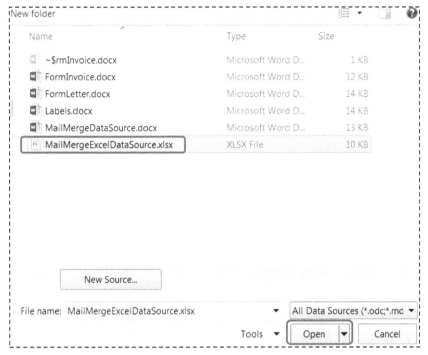

8. Click the '**Open**' button

A prompt similar to the following will appear:

9. Verify the radio button '**Show all**' is selected

10. Select '**MS Excel Worksheets via DDE (*.xls)**'

11. Click the '**OK**' button

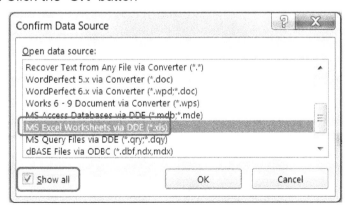

The following prompt will appear:

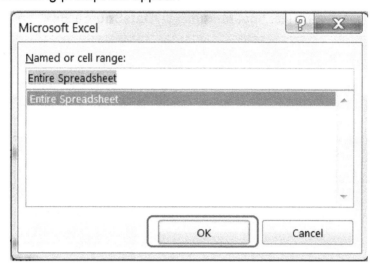

12. Click the **'OK'** button

13. Place your cursor in from front of the word **'Dear'**

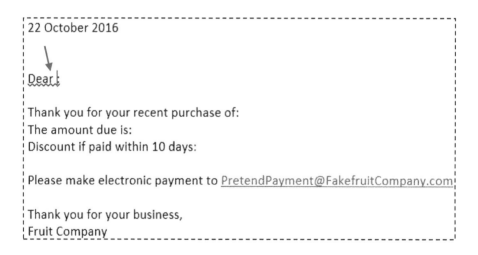

14. From the **'MAILINGS'** tab select the **'Insert Merge Field'** drop-down box

15. Select **'FirstName'** (*should be inserted after the word 'Dear'*)

16. After **'FirstName'** press your **'Spacebar'** on your keyboard

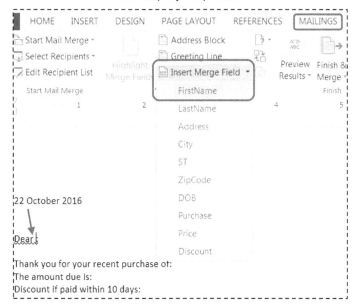

17. From the **'Insert Merge Field'** drop-down box Select **'LastName'** (*should be inserted after FirstName and space*)

18. Place your cursor after the words **'purchase of:'** and press your **'Spacebar'** on your keyboard

19. From the **'Insert Merge Field'** drop-down box Select **'Purchase'** (*should be inserted after the colon :*) optionally you may also apply bold formatting to the merged field **<<Purchase>>**

20. Repeat steps 18 & 19 for merge fields **<<Price>>** and **<<Discount>>**

21. Save the file **(CTRL + S)**

MERGING THE INVOICE

1. With the **'FormInvoice'** document open, select the **'MAILINGS'** tab

2. Select the **'Finish & Merge'** drop-down box and then **'Edit Individual Documents…'**

The following prompt should appear:

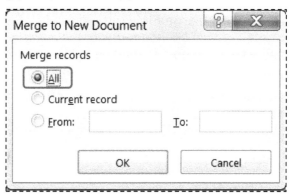

3. If not already selected, select the **'All'** radio button and click the **'OK'** button

A new word document should now be created

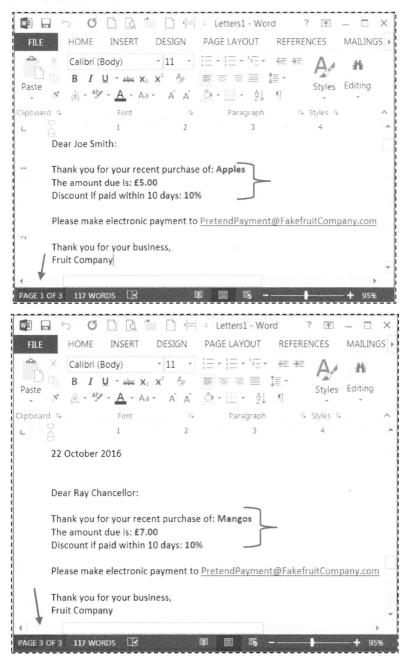

Review the merged document, if the results are as you expected them to be, you may *rename and save* the file or *print out* each invoice for distribution.

CHAPTER 6
Email Merge Messages

For our last two examples we'll demonstrate how to create Mail Merge email messages. Personalized email messages can be a great way to communicate with customers or employees. However, unlike creating items that must be printed to distribute, such as form letters, invoices, labels etc., email messages are sent electronically, therefore it is very important to preview and test your Mail Merge email before mass sending.

To save time we'll re-use the records contained in the **'MailMergeDataSource.docx'** file.

> In order to complete this exercise, you will need
> **Microsoft® Outlook®** or **Windows® Live® Mail®**
> installed on your computer.

EMAIL EXAMPLE
For our first example, we'll create an email similar to the form letter we created in Chapter 3, only this time the merged element will be an email instead of a letter.

CREATING THE DATA SOURCE FILE
STEP-BY-STEP EXAMPLE:
1. Open the **C:\MailMergeTraining** folder and select the file: **'MailMergeDataSource.docx'**
2. In the column currently labeled **'ST'**, change to **'Email'**
3. Delete the **'ST'**, contents for each row
   - NY - *Delete*
   - CA - *Delete*
   - WA – *Delete*

The result should look similar to the following:

FirstName	LastName	Address	City	Email	ZipCode	DOB
Joe	Smith	123 State Street	New York		10001	05/01/1975
Sally	Williams	321 Main Street	Los Angeles		90008	11/18/1985
Ray	Chancellor	222 University Ave	Seattle		98001	02/25/1969

4. For the email addresses you may enter the following **_or_** use your own email for **testing in this exercise**.
   - bentontrainingbooks@gmail.com
   - cj1999c@yahoo.com
   - <reader's email address>

DO NOT USE real employee or customer email addresses

FirstName	LastName	Address	City	Email
Joe	Smith	123 State Street	New York	bentontrainingbooks@gmail.com
Sally	Williams	321 Main Street	Los Angeles	cj1999c@yahoo.com
Ray	Chancellor	222 University Ave	Seattle	

5. Save the file in the folder **MailMergeTraining (CTRL + S)** name it **MailMergeEmailDataSource.docx**

6. Close the file

CREATING THE MAIL MESSAGE

1. Open the file **'FormLetter.docx'**

2. When the SQL prompt appears click 'No':

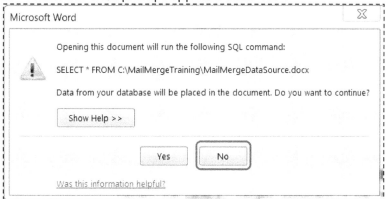

3. Delete the previous merge fields:
   - «FirstName»
   - «LastName»
   - «Address»
   - «DOB»

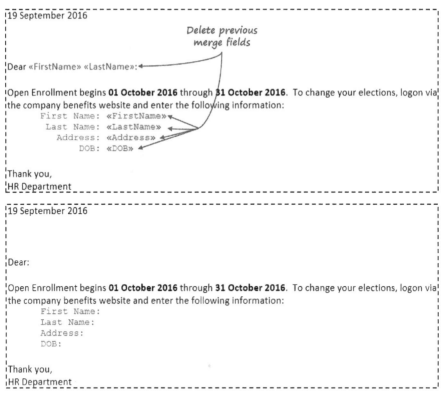

4. Save the file in the folder **MailMergeTraining (CTRL + S)** name it **EmailMessage.docx**

5. From the Ribbon select **MAILINGS : Select Recipients : Us̲e an Existing List…**

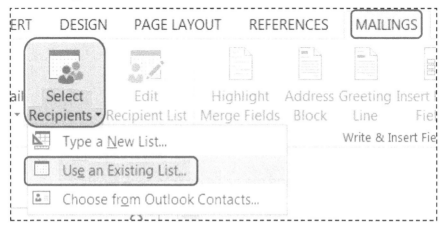

6. When prompted, open the **C:\MailMergeTraining** folder

7. Select the file: **'MailMergeEmailDataSource.docx'**

8. Apply each Merge Field by selecting from the **'MAILINGS'** tab, the **'Insert Merge Field'** drop-down box

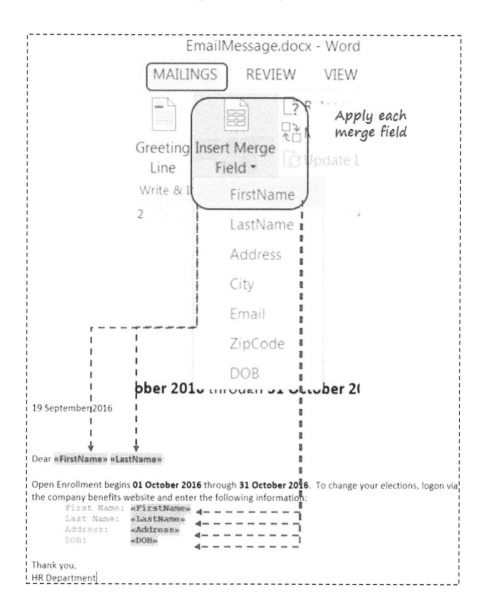

9. Save file **(CTRL + S)**

MERGING THE EMAIL MESSAGE

1. With Microsoft® Outlook® open

2. With the **'EmailMessge.docx'** document open, select the **'MAILINGS'** tab

3. Select 'Preview Results'

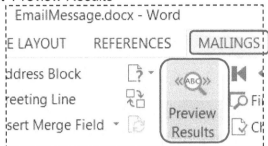

A result similar to the following should now be displayed:

4. Verify message text is correct

5. Double check email addresses are correct on the Data Source file

6. With the **'EmailMessge.docx'** document open, select the **'MAILINGS'** tab

7. Select the **'Finish & Merge'** drop-down box and then **'Send Email Messages…'**

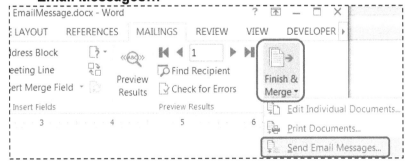

8. The following prompt will appear, in the **'Subject line:'** box enter the following text:
   - Mail Merge Test Exercise (Chapter 6)

9. If not already selected, select the **'All'** radio button and click the **'OK'** button

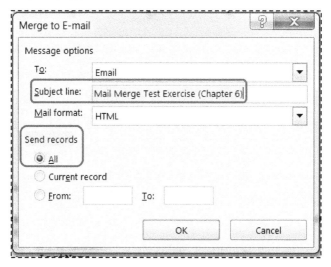

10. Check your email '**Inbox'** for the test message

11. You may also check your **'Sent'** folder to view the messages sent

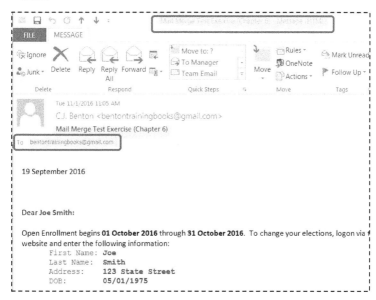

OUTLOOK® CONTACTS EXAMPLE

In the previous examples, we used a Data Source *file* (either Microsoft® Word® or Excel®). However, you may also use source fields contained in the Outlook® Contacts feature to create merged messages.

Let's say you were a company and wanted to verify new customer profile information, you could use Mail Merge as a quick way to send verification messages or requests for additional information.

For example, if your company had an automated process in which customers who placed their first order were automatically added to a customer service managed Outlook® Contacts list. You could then create a tailored email message to all new customers verifying their account information.

To illustrate this feature, I will walk through the process, even if you do not have similar information already contained in your Outlook® Contacts to complete this exercise, you will still be able to follow along to understand how this functionality works.

CREATING THE OUTLOOK® CONTACTS MAIL MESSAGE

1. Open Microsoft® Outlook®
2. Open Microsoft® Word®
3. Create a new blank Word® document **(CTRL + N)**
4. Type the following text information:

Dear :

The Fruit Company looks forward to having you as a valued client! To ensure we provide you with the highest level of service, please *provide* or *verify* the following information, simply click **'Reply'** to complete:

```
First Name:
Last Name:
Title:
Email:
Web Address:
```

Thank you,
Fruit Company Customer Service Team

---

5. Save the Word® document to: **C:\MailMergeTraining**

6. Name the email text document:
   'EmailMessge_Contacts.docx'

7. From the Ribbon select **MAILINGS : Select Recipients : Choose from Outlook Contacts...**

A prompt *similar* to the following should appear:

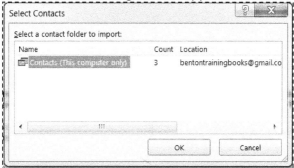

8. Click the **'OK'** button

A prompt *similar* to the following should appear, the fields may display in a *different order* (*i.e. Last, First, Title, Company etc.*)

9. Select the recipients you would like to send the email message to

10. Click the **'OK'** button

Next apply the Merge Fields by selecting the **'MAILINGS'** tab then the **'Insert Merge Field'** drop-down box.

Please Note: *these fields match the Outlook® contact fields.*

Dear **«First» «Last»**:

The Fruit Company looks forward to having you as valued client! To ensure we provide you with the highest level of service, please *provide* or *verify* the following information, simply click **'Reply'** to complete:

```
First Name:    «First»
Last Name:     «Last»
Title:         «Job_Title»
Email:         «Email_Address»
Web Address:   «Web_Page»
```

Thank you,
Fruit Company Customer Service Team

MERGING THE OUTLOOK® CONTACTS MAIL MESSAGE

1. With Microsoft® Outlook® open

2. With the **'EmailMessge_Contacts.docx'** document open, select the **'MAILINGS'** tab

3. Select 'Preview Results'

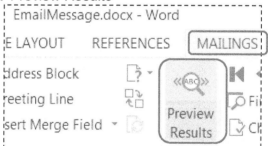

4. Verify message text is correct

Dear C. Benton:

The Fruit Company looks forward to having you as a valued client! To ensure we provide you with the highest level of service, please *provide* or *verify* the following information, simply click **'Reply'** to complete:

```
First Name:    C.
Last Name:     Benton
Title:         Author
Email:         bentontrainingbooks@gmail.com
Web Address:   http://bentonexcelbooks.my-free.website/
```

Thank you,
Fruit Company Customer Service Team

5. Select the **'Finish & Merge'** drop-down box and then **'Send Email Messages…'**

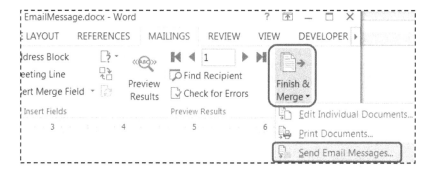

6. The following prompt will appear, in the **'Subject line:'** box enter the following text:
   - Welcome to the Fruit Company - Customer Verification

   a. In this example, since it is *customer facing*, a good best practice after previewing the current record is to select the **'Current record'** radio button

   b. Click the **'OK'** button

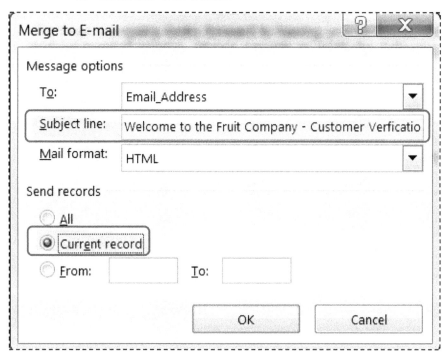

7. Check your email **'Sent'** folder to view the message, if the email appears correct, you can send to all recipients by repeating step #12 and selecting the **'All'** radio button *(instead of **'Current record')** and then the **'OK'** button.

OTHER BOOKS AVAILABLE BY THIS AUTHOR:

1. Microsoft® Excel® Start Here The Beginners Guide

2. The Step-By-Step Guide To The 25 Most Common Microsoft® Excel® Formulas & Features

3. The Step-By-Step Guide To Pivot Tables & Introduction To Dashboards

4. The Step-By-Step Guide To The VLOOKUP formula in Microsoft® Excel®

5. The Microsoft® Excel® Step-By-Step Training Guide Book Bundle

6. Excel® Macros & VBA For Business Users - A Beginners Guide

www.ingramcontent.com/pod-product-compliance
Lightning Source LLC
Chambersburg PA
CBHW070900070326
40690CB00009B/1933